Amici

Edexcel GCSE Exam Guide

Carole Shepherd   **Derek Aust**

OXFORD

UNIVERSITY PRESS

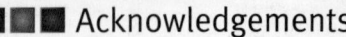

The Publisher would like to thank the following for permission to reproduce photographs: Authors: pp.20, 21, 33, 35; Stockbyte: p.28.

The authors would like to thank their families for their helpful support, suggestions and encouragement, in particular Vasilija Aust and Caterina McKillop.

The Publisher would like to thank Luisa Carrer (language consultant).

OXFORD
UNIVERSITY PRESS

Great Clarendon Street, Oxford OX2 6DP

Oxford University Press is a department of the University of Oxford.
It furthers the University's objective of excellence in research, scholarship,
and education by publishing worldwide in

Oxford   New York
Auckland   Cape Town   Dar es Salaam   Hong Kong   Karachi
Kuala Lumpur   Madrid   Melbourne   Mexico City   Nairobi
New Delhi   Shanghai   Taipei   Toronto

With offices in

Argentina   Austria   Brazil   Chile   Czech Republic   France   Greece
Guatemala   Hungary   Italy   Japan   South Korea   Poland   Portugal
Singapore   Switzerland   Thailand   Turkey   Ukraine   Vietnam

Oxford is a registered trade mark of Oxford University Press
in the UK and in certain other countries

British Library Cataloguing in Publication Data

Data available

ISBN 978 019 913515 8

3 5 7 9 10 8 6 4 2

Designed and typeset by John Dickinson – Design for Print

Printed in Great Britain by Ashford Colour Press Ltd

Contents ■■■■■

How to use this booklet

The *Amici* coursebook and workbook really provide all that you need to get a good grade in Italian GCSE, provided you use them wisely! This *Amici* Exam Guide gives you extra practice in Speaking and Writing as well as Listening and Reading for Edexcel examinations and reminds you of useful pages in *Amici* which you should also refer to for revision.

Part 1: Speaking and Writing

The topics listed in this booklet are those stipulated by Edexcel but you may choose a context/purpose of your own. As Speaking and Writing tasks will be set by your teachers, we thought you would find it useful to have a list of some important words and expressions from *Amici* as well as a reminder of important grammar points that you may need to use when preparing for these tasks. Remember: once you start preparing your tasks, your teacher cannot give you any help, so it is important you know how to use *Amici* and other resources wisely. You will need to show you know a lot of grammar, vocabulary and expressions related to the task. A full list of the vocabulary and expressions used in *Amici* (in Italian and English) can also be found at the following website: www.oup.com/oxed/secondary/mfl/amici/

Part 2: Listening and Reading

You will be entered for either Foundation or Higher examinations. In this booklet tasks are identified as **F** (Foundation), **H** (Higher) or **F/H** (Foundation/Higher), but we recommend you try all of the activities so that you get lots of practice with different vocabulary and tasks.

To help with your revision for the Listening examinations we have chosen a selection of recordings from *Amici* which relate to the Edexcel topics and created different exercises for them. For revision purposes you have personal control of the CD included with this exam guide, so will be able to listen as many times as you like. You will be able to check your answers in the back of this booklet, but please make sure you do this AFTER you have done the exercise! All the transcripts are included on the CD ROM.

The Reading comprehension texts and exercises are all new but you should recognise some of the vocabulary. These texts have also been designed to give you some useful expressions to help you with your Speaking and Writing tasks.

Icons

Edexcel uses lots of visual icons in Listening and Reading examination papers, but we do not have enough space to include these here. Instead, you have a good range of exercise types to practise. Ask your teacher to give you some Edexcel past papers so that you can get used to the icons they use!

Edexcel Requirements

Unit 1: Listening and Understanding in Italian (20%)

Foundation Tier: 25 minutes (+ 5 minutes reading time)
Higher Tier: 35 minutes (+ 5 minutes reading time)

This unit will test vocabulary and structures from the four common topic areas (listed in Part 2 of this book). You are given 5 minutes at the beginning of the test to read the questions. Then you will hear each item twice, with pauses following the second hearing to allow you time to write your answers and to read the next question before the next extract is played. There will be a range of question types, requiring non-verbal responses or responses in English.

Unit 2: Speaking in Italian (30%)

Controlled Assessment (internally assessed)

The Speaking tasks will be chosen by your teacher and will relate to one or more of these themes: *media and culture, sport and leisure, travel and tourism* or *business, work and employment* or *a centre-devised option*. You will be assessed under controlled conditions on **two** speaking activities chosen from these task types: an open interaction, a picture-based free-flowing discussion or a presentation with discussion. Each activity must last for 4–6 minutes. You cannot submit the same task for both Speaking and Writing but the theme can be the same as that chosen for Unit 4.

Unit 3: Reading and Understanding in Italian (20%)

Foundation Tier: 35 minutes

Higher Tier: 50 minutes

This unit draws on vocabulary and structures from the four common topic areas (listed in Part 2 of this book). There will be a variety of tasks which require a written or non-verbal response. The examination will include a number of short texts, notices or news reports in Italian which include a range of settings and formal/informal styles (e.g. text messages, advertisements, e-mails).

Unit 4: Writing in Italian (30%)

Controlled Assessment (externally assessed)

The focus of the writing unit will be chosen by your teacher and will relate to one or more of the themes listed in Unit 2 (and Part 1 of this book). You cannot submit the same task for both Speaking and Writing but the theme can be the same as that chosen for Unit 2. You will have to complete **two** separate writing tasks under controlled conditions. You should produce at least 100 words in each of the two assessment sessions. Students aiming for grade C or above are expected to produce over 200 words in each task.

1 Media and culture

Music/film/reading/fashion/celebrities/religion/blogs/internet

(Non) mi piacciono …	*I (don't) like …*
i cartoni animati	*cartoons*
i documentari	*documentaries*
i teleromanzi	*TV soaps*
i programmi sportivi	*sports programmes*
i programmi di attualità	*current affairs programmes*
i programmi sulla natura	*nature programmes*
i programmi di cucina	*cooking programmes*
i film d'amore	*love films*
i film d'avventura	*adventure films*
i film d'azione	*action films*
i film comici	*comic films*
i film di guerra	*war films*
i film polizieschi	*adventure films*
i film romantici	*romantic films*
i film dell'orrore	*horror films*
i film di spionaggio	*spy films*
i film di fantascienza	*science fiction films*
i film western	*westerns*

Il film era ambientato in città negli anni 1990	*The film was set in a town in the 1990s*
Il film/il libro trattava di un ragazzo che incontra …	*The film/the book was about a boy who meets …*
Il film era violento/tragico	*The film was violent/tragic*
Il film era bello	*The film was beautiful*
Il film era commovente	*The film was moving*
Gli effetti speciali erano incredibili	*The special effects were incredible*
Gli attori erano bravi	*The actors were good*
Gli attori erano eccellenti	*The actors were excellent*
I personaggi principali erano poco credibili	*The main characters were not very credible*
La trama era complicata	*The plot was complicated*

Try using some of these expressions to describe a film you have seen recently, e.g. *Il film era ambientato in montagna. Era molto tragico. I personaggi principali erano interessanti e gli attori erano bravi. La trama era molto complicata ma gli effetti speciali erano fantastici.*

➔ Useful pages in *Amici*: 124–125

Mi piace molto ... fin da quando ero piccola	*Since I was little I have loved ...*
Per me la canzone più bella è stata ...	*The best song for me was ...*
Per me è una delle voci più belle della storia della musica	*For me he/she has got one of the most beautiful voices in the history of music*
Ha una voce molto profonda	*He/she has a really deep voice*
Il recentissimo fenomeno pop di grande qualità	*The newest top quality pop phenomenon*
A mio parere è bravissimo/a	*In my opinion he/she is great*
Ha una voce magnifica	*He/she has a wonderful voice*

Try using some of these expressions to describe an artist you like, e.g. *Si tratta di Leona Lewis, nuovissimo fenomeno pop soul di grande qualità di soli 21 anni, vincitrice della terza edizione del talent show "X Factor".*

La Moda

l'abbigliamento	*clothing*	la maglietta	*t-shirt*
l'abito	*suit, dress*	gli orecchini	*earrings*
andare di moda	*to be in fashion*	i pantaloni	*trousers*
la borsa	*bag, handbag*	il portafoglio	*wallet*
la calza	*stocking*	il portamonete	*purse*
i calzini	*socks*	il piercing	*piercing*
la camicia	*shirt*	il profumo	*perfume*
la camicetta	*blouse*	il pullover	*pullover*
il costume da bagno	*bathing costume*	il sandalo	*sandal*
la cravatta	*tie*	la scarpa	*shoe*
la felpa	*sweatshirt*	la sciarpa	*scarf*
la giacca	*jacket*	lo stivale	*boot*
la gonna	*skirt*	il tatuaggio	*tattoo*
i jeans (inv)	*jeans*	il vestito	*dress*
la maglia	*jumper*	i vestiti	*clothes*

Try using some of these words to describe what sort of fashion you like, e.g. *Se un vestito mi piace lo compro anche se non è alla moda. Mi piacerebbe un tatuaggio o un piercing, ma la mamma non ne sarebbe contenta!*

➜ Useful pages in *Amici*: 128–129

A quick reminder:

Nouns	**Adjectives**

Nouns

Italian nouns end in **-o**, **-a** or **-e**. In the plural these endings change as follows:

-o	-i
-a	-e
-e	-i

libro ⟶ libri
penna ⟶ penne
cellulare ⟶ cellulari

Adjectives

Italian adjectives ending in **-o** have four forms. Those ending in **-e** have two forms.

-o	-i
-a	-e
-e	-i

italiano ⟶ italiani
italiana ⟶ italiane
inglese ⟶ inglesi

NB: tedesco/a ⟶ tedeschi/e

The present tense

Regular verb infinitives end in **-are**, **-ere** or **-ire**.

-are	-ere	-ire (1)	-ire (2)
-o	-o	-o	-isco
-i	-i	-i	-isci
-a	-e	-e	-isce
-iamo	-iamo	-iamo	-iamo
-ate	-ete	-ite	-ite
-ano	-ono	-ono	-iscono

NB: **-care** and **-gare** verbs add an 'h' before 'e' or 'i':
cercare ⟶ cerco, cerchi etc.;
pagare ⟶ pago, pag<u>h</u>i etc.

-iare verbs drop the 'i' in the **tu** form unless it is stressed:
viaggiare ⟶ viaggi;
cominciare ⟶ cominci; but
sciare: sc<u>ii</u>.

The perfect tense

For the perfect tense you need the present tense of **avere (ho, hai, ha, abbiamo, avete, hanno)** or **essere** and the past participle of the verb. For the past participle of regular verbs, take off the **-are**, **-ere** or **-ire** and add the ending:

-are	-ato	lavorare	⟶	lavorato
-ere	-uto	vendere	⟶	venduto
-ire	-ito	finire	⟶	finito

Most verbs take **avere (ho, hai, ha, abbiamo, avete, hanno)**
e.g. **ho lavorato, ho venduto, ho finito**.

Some verbs take **essere (sono, sei, è, siamo, siete, sono)**
e.g. andare, arrivare, essere (stato), nascere (nato), morire (morto), piacere (piaciuto), rimanere (rimasto), stare, uscire, venire (venuto).

The past participle of verbs taking **essere** agrees with the subject
e.g. Marco: "sono andato", Daniela: "sono andata"; i miei amici sono andati; le mie amiche sono andate.

The imperfect tense

To form the imperfect, remove the **-re** of the infinitive and add:
-vo, *-vi*, *-va*, *-vamo*, *-vate*, *-vano* e.g. stavo; avevo; finivo.

NB: **fare**: facevo; facevi; faceva; facevamo; facevate; facevano.

essere: ero; eri; era; eravamo; eravate; erano.

➔ Useful pages in *Amici*: 26–27, 68–69, 210–211, 214, 216, 225–227

Expressing the future

As in English, there are many ways of avoiding the future tense in Italian, e.g. use the present tense or an expression such as **Ho intenzione di/ Spero di/Vorrei**.
Ho intenzione di sposarmi all'età di 30 anni.
Spero di avere due bambini. Vorrei vivere in Italia.

The future tense

The future endings are: **-ò, -ai, -à, -emo, -ete, -anno**.

Regular **-ere** and **-ire** verbs form the future tense 'stem' by removing the final 'e' of the infinitive. Regular **-are** verbs change the 'a' of the infinitive to 'e': parlar ⟶ parler.

parlare	parlerò	parlerai	parlerà	parleremo	parlerete	parleranno
vendere	venderò	venerai	venderà	venderemo	venderete	venderanno
finire	finirò	finirai	finirà	finiremo	finirete	finiranno

NB: **-care** and **-gare** verbs add an '**h**' throughout:
cercare ⟶ cercherò etc.; pagare ⟶ pagherò etc.

-giare verbs and most **-ciare** verbs drop the '**i**':
viaggiare ⟶ viaggerò; cominciare ⟶ comincerò

A number of verbs have the same endings but a different "stem":
andare ⟶ andrò; fare ⟶ farò; potere ⟶ potrò.

The only completely irregular verb stem is **essere**:
sarò, sarai, sarà, saremo, sarete, saranno.

The conditional tense

The conditional tense has the same "stem" as the future but these endings: **-ei, -esti, -ebbe, -emmo, -este, -ebbero**.

Any verb which is irregular in the future will also be irregular in the conditional e.g. **essere: sarei, saresti, sarebbe, saremmo, sareste, sarebbero**.

e.g. Mangio tutto quello che non **dovrei** mangiare.
Vorrei mangiare più frutta.
Mi piacerebbe andare in palestra.

➜ Useful pages in *Amici*: 48, 116–117, 217, 225–227

aiuto !

When preparing for your Writing or Speaking tasks, try to use a variety of tenses, time expressions, vocabulary and adjectives. Adapt the sentences in this Chapter, e.g.

Andavo in palestra spesso.	past
Vado in piscina ogni giorno.	present
Andrò allo stadio giovedì prossimo.	future

2 Sport and leisure

Hobbies/interests/sporting events/lifestyle choices

Preferisco il calcio	*I prefer football*
Odio giocare a calcio	*I hate playing football*
Mi piace giocare a hockey	*I like to play hockey*
Guardo la partita allo stadio	*I watch the match at the stadium*
Preferisco guardare la partita alla televisione	*I prefer watching the match on television*
Non mi piace andare a cavallo	*I don't like horse riding*
Detesto andare in palestra	*I hate going to the gym*
Odio andare al centro sportivo	*I hate going to the sports centre*
È fantastico	*It's fantastic*
È molto interessante	*It's very interesting*
È abbastanza pericoloso	*It's quite dangerous*
È un po' noioso	*It's a little boring*

Mi piace ...	*I like ...*
giocare nel parco	*playing in the park*
giocare a carte	*playing cards*
suonare la chitarra	*playing the guitar*
ascoltare la musica	*listening to music*
guardare la tv	*watching TV*
leggere i giornali, le riviste	*reading papers, magazines*
passeggiare con il cane	*walking the dog*
andare al cinema, a teatro	*going to the cinema, theatre*
andare ai concerti	*going to concerts*
andare in città/disco(teca)	*going to town/the disco*
andare in campagna	*going to the country(side)*
uscire con amici	*going out with friends*
chiacchierare con amici	*chatting with friends*

Try using some of these words to describe what you like to do in your free time. Add some connectives and time expressions, e.g. *Guardo la partita di calcio ogni sabato allo stadio, e poi vado in città con gli amici. Andiamo spesso a mangiare una pizza prima di andare al cinema o in discoteca.*

Il mio passatempo preferito è uscire con gli amici. È un po' noioso uscire da solo/a! Quando sei con gli amici puoi chiacchierare oppure ascoltare la musica insieme.

➜ Useful pages in *Amici*: 20–25, 120–125, 184

Quando ero più giovane — *When I was younger*

Volevo mantenermi in forma	*I wanted to keep fit*
Camminavo ogni giorno	*I used to walk every day*
Mi piaceva fare footing	*I used to like jogging*
Andavo in palestra	*I used to go to the gym*
Giocavo a calcio	*I used to play football*
Andavo in piscina	*I used to go to the pool*

Adesso — *Now*

Ho cominciato a giocare a …	*I started playing …*
Ho smesso di giocare a …	*I stopped playing …*
Ho smesso di fumare	*I have stopped smoking*
Non gioco più a calcio	*I no longer play football*
Non vado più in palestra	*I no longer go to the gym*
A colazione mangio poco	*I don't eat much breakfast*

Per tenermi in forma … — *To keep myself fit …*

Sto attento alla dieta	*I look after my diet*
Bevo molta acqua	*I drink a lot of water*
Cerco di evitare i cibi grassi	*I try to avoid fatty foods*
Mangio frutta e verdura	*I eat fruit and vegetables*
Vado in bicicletta	*I go by bicycle*
Faccio molto sport	*I do a lot of sport*
Non vado a letto tardi	*I don't go to bed late*
Non bevo alcolici	*I don't drink alcohol*
Non fumo (più)	*I don't smoke (any more)*

In futuro — *In the future*

Andrò in palestra	*I'll go to the gym*
Farò aerobica	*I'll do aerobics*
Mangerò più frutta	*I'll eat more fruit*

Expressions of time:

una volta alla settimana	*once a week*
due volte al mese	*twice a month*
due ore al giorno	*two hours a day*
durante la settimana	*during the week*
ogni giorno/sera	*every day/evening*
ogni venerdì	*every Friday*
ogni tanto	*every now and then*
ogni due o tre giorni	*every two or three days*
qualche volta	*sometimes*
spesso	*often*

Try using different tenses and expressions of time,
e.g. *Andavo in palestra **una volta alla settimana**.*
*Adesso ci vado solo **ogni tanto**.*
*La settimana prossima andrò in palestra **ogni sera**!*
*Mi mantengo **spesso** in forma.*

➜ Useful pages in *Amici*: 20–25, 41, 106–109

A quick reminder:

Relative pronouns

A **relative pronoun** refers back to someone/something that has just been mentioned.

1. **che** means who, whom, which, that and is invariable.
   L'unico sport <u>che</u> mi piace è il calcio.
   The only sport that I like is football.
   Se c'è qualcosa <u>che</u> mi piace lo prendo.
   If there is something I like, I'll get it.

2. **cui** is usually used with a preposition (to/in which, to/from whom etc.) and is invariable.
   Questo è l'albergo <u>in cui</u> ho incontrato i miei amici.
   This is the hotel in which I met my friends.
   Ecco la piazza <u>di cui</u> ti ho parlato.
   Here is the square about which I spoke to you.

3. **cui** can also mean "whose".
   Quella amica, <u>il cui nome</u> non ricordo, è italiana.
   The friend, whose name I do not remember, is Italian.

➔ Useful pages in *Amici*: 77, 91, 175, 221

Subjunctive expressions

The present subjunctive is sometimes needed after certain expressions e.g. **Penso che/È importante che:**
Penso che sia una buona idea
I think it is a good idea
L'importante è che sia sempre qualcosa di elegante.
The important thing is that it is always elegant.

The imperfect subjunctive is frequently used after **se** (if) to express the idea of something you would like to happen.
Se <u>avessi</u> la possibilità di viaggiare, andrei in Italia.
If I could travel, I'd go to Italy.
Se <u>fossi</u> ricco farei una bella vacanza.
If I was rich I'd have a lovely holiday.

➔ Useful pages in *Amici*: 174, 219–220

aiuto !

When preparing for your Writing or Speaking tasks, try to use a variety of tenses, time expressions, vocabulary and adjectives. Adapt the sentences in this Chapter, e.g.

Quando ero giovane, l'unico sport <u>che</u> mi piaceva era la pallacanestro.

Penso che la moda italiana <u>sia</u> molto bella.

Se <u>fossi</u> ricco/a andrei a vivere in America.

Comparison of adjectives

1. Comparatives

più ... di	more ... than	(tanto) ...quanto	as ... as
meno ... di	less ... than	(così) ... come	as ... as

Daniela è più vecchia di Stefano.
Daniela is older than Stefano.

Firenze è (così) bella come Roma.
Florence is as beautiful as Rome.

Some regular and irregular comparative forms:

buono good; **più buono/migliore** better
cattivo bad; **più cattivo/peggiore** worse
grande big; **più grande/maggiore** bigger
piccolo small; **più piccolo/minore** smaller

2. Superlatives

il più / la più (the most) **il meno / la meno** (the least)

For: 'Florence is the most beautiful city' you can say:
Firenze è la più bella città or **Firenze è la città più bella.**

Some regular and irregular superlative forms:
il più buono/il migliore the best
il più cattivo/il peggiore the worst
il più grande/il maggiore the biggest
il più piccolo/il minore the smallest
Il maggiore vantaggio di Internet è ...
The biggest advantage of the Internet is ...

For "very ..." you can add **-issimo** to the adjective:
Pisa è bellissima. Pisa is very beautiful.

Some regular and irregular superlative forms:
buonissimo/ottimo very good
cattivissimo/pessimo very bad
grandissimo/massimo very big
piccolissimo/minimo very small

➜ Useful pages in *Amici*: 61, 212

aiuto !

When preparing for your Writing or Speaking tasks, try to use a variety of tenses, time expressions, vocabulary and adjectives. Adapt the sentences in this Chapter, e.g.

Marco è <u>più alto</u> di Daniela.

Roma è <u>la più bella</u> capitale d'Europa.

Il calcio è un gioco <u>interessantissimo</u>!

3 Travel and tourism

Holidays/accommodation/eating, food, drink

Di solito passo una settimana al mare	*Usually I spend a week at the seaside*
Mi sembra una vacanza ideale	*It seems an ideal holiday*
Passo una quindicina di giorni in montagna	*I spend a fortnight in the mountains*
Mi piace stare in albergo	*I like staying in a hotel*
Fare campeggio è meno caro che stare in albergo	*Camping is less expensive than staying in a hotel*
Preferisco affittare un appartamento	*I prefer to rent an apartment*
Vado a trovare amici	*I go to see friends*
Posso rilassarmi	*I can relax*
Ho intenzione di partire verso la fine di agosto	*I intend to leave towards the end of August*
Mi piace fare delle belle passeggiate	*I like going for nice walks*
Mi piace prendere il sole	*I like to sunbathe*
Non vedo l'ora di andare in vacanza	*I can't wait to go on holiday*
C'è qualcosa da fare per persone di tutte le età	*There is something to do for people of all ages*
Sono andato in vacanza con amici	*I went on holiday with friends*
L'estate scorsa ho viaggiato in treno	*Last summer I travelled by train*
Ho fatto campeggio	*I went camping*
Ho incontrato giovani di tutte le parti del mondo	*I met young people from all over the world*
Ho passato il tempo a prendere il sole	*I spent time sunbathing*
Ho visitato tanti musei	*I visited lots of museums*
Ho visto tanto	*I saw so much*
Ho fatto lo sci nautico	*I went water skiing*
Sono andato a pescare ogni giorno	*Every day I went fishing*
Mi sono divertito un mondo	*I really enjoyed myself*
Era fantastico	*It was fantastic*
Faceva bello ma non troppo caldo	*It was nice weather but not too hot*
Se avessi la possibilità di viaggiare andrei in Italia	*If I could travel, I'd go to Italy*
Se fossi ricco farei una bella vacanza	*If I was rich I'd have a lovely holiday*
Mi piacerebbe andare in un'isola disabitata	*I'd like to go to a desert island*

→ Useful pages in *Amici*: 60–67

Ha una camera libera per favore?	*Have you a room free, please?*
C'è l'ascensore?	*Is there a lift?*
È inclusa la colazione?	*Is breakfast included?*
Quanto costa la camera con bagno?	*How much does a room with a bath cost?*
Posso prenotare la camera?	*Can I book the room?*
Posso portare il cane?	*Can I bring the dog?*
Vorrei una camera a due letti con doccia	*I would like a twin bedded room with a shower*
Desidero la camera e la prima colazione	*I would like bed and breakfast*
Dal … luglio al … agosto	*From … July to … August*
Per dieci notti	*For ten nights*
C'è ancora posto per una tenda/ un camper?	*Is there still room for a tent/a camper van?*
C'è un campo da tennis?	*Is there a tennis court?*
C'è una lavanderia?	*Is there a laundry?*
C'è una piazzuola per una roulotte?	*Is there space for a caravan?*
Ci sono docce con acqua calda?	*Are there showers with hot water?*
Posso affittare uno chalet?	*Can I book a chalet?*
Posso noleggiare una tenda?	*Can I hire a tent?*
Abbiamo la moto	*We have a motor bike*
Siamo due adulti e un ragazzo	*We are two adults and a child (m)*
Vogliamo fermarci due notti	*We want to stay two nights*
Abbiamo la macchina	*We have a car*
A me non piace il formaggio	*I do not like cheese*
Prendo un panino al prosciutto/ formaggio	*I'll have a ham/cheese sandwich*
Da mangiare niente, grazie	*Nothing to eat, thank you*
Come antipasto prendo il melone	*I'll have melon for starters*
Per primo prendiamo spaghetti	*We'll have spaghetti for the first course*
Per secondo vorrei vitello arrosto	*I would like roast veal for the main course*
Per contorno mi porti una porzione di patate fritte	*Bring me a portion of chips as a side dish*
Per dolce ci porti frutta di stagione	*Bring us seasonal fruits as a sweet*
Mi può portare il conto?	*Can you bring me the bill?*

A quick reminder:

The passive

The passive is formed when the object of the sentence becomes the subject. Compare these two sentences:

Le macchine inquinano l'aria. Cars pollute <u>the air</u>. (object)

L'aria è inquinata dalle macchine.
<u>The air</u> (subject) is polluted by cars. (passive)

In Italian the passive can be used in all tenses. You need the verb **essere** + the past participle of the verb. The past participle(s) must agree with the subject e.g.

present (minacciare)	future
è minacciato/a	sarà minacciato/a
sono minacciati/e	saranno minacciati/e
imperfect	**perfect**
era minacciato/a	è stato/a minacciato/a
erano minacciati/e	sono stati/e minacciati/e

La nostra salute è minacciata dall'inquinamento.
Our health <u>is</u> threatened by pollution.

La nostra salute è <u>stata</u> minacciata dall'inquinamento.
Our health <u>has been</u> threatened by pollution.

La nostra salute <u>era</u> minacciata dall'inquinamento.
Our health <u>was</u> threatened by pollution.

La nostra salute <u>sarà</u> minacciata dall'inquinamento.
Our health <u>will be</u> threatened by pollution.

You can avoid the passive in Italian by using:
* **si** + the third person singular/plural of the verb:
Si vedono graffiti dappertutto. Graffiti can be seen everywhere.

* the active form of the verb:
L'inquinamento minaccia la nostra salute.
Pollution is threatening our health.

Impersonal verbs

Impersonal verbs have the subject 'it' or 'there' not 'I, you' etc. Frequently used impersonal constructions start with è:

È essenziale/importante/necessario riciclare tutto.
It is essential/important/necessary to recycle.

È meglio usare I mezzi pubblici. It is better to use public transport.

A common impersonal verb is **bisogna (bisognare)** 'it is necessary' and it is only used in this form.

Bisogna riciclare i nostri rifiuti. It is necessary to recycle our rubbish.

➔ Useful pages in *Amici*: 149, 150, 153, 214, 219

Adapt some of the sentences in this Chapter to include the passive and/or impersonal verbs. Add some connectives.

La nostra salute è minacciata dall'inquinamento, perciò è importante aiutare l'ambiente.

Pronouns

subj.	reflex.	dir. object	ind. object	emphatic
io	mi	mi	mi	me
tu	ti	ti	ti	te
lui	si	lo	gli	lui
lei	si	la	le	lei
Lei	si	La	Le	Lei
noi	ci	ci	ci	noi
voi	vi	vi	vi	voi
loro	si	li	loro/gli	loro
Loro	si	Le	Loro/gli	Loro

Subject pronouns are only used for clarity or emphasis.
Io vado in bicicletta ma lui va in macchina.
I go by bike, but he goes by car.

Reflexive pronouns are used with reflexive verbs.
La mia casa si trova in periferia.
My house is situated on the outskirts.

Direct object pronouns are normally placed in front of the verb and agree with the noun they replace.
Vedi la zona pedonale? No, non la vedo.
Can you see the pedestrian zone? No, I can't see it.
Le piste ciclabili? Le ho già viste.
The cycle lanes? I have already seen them.

Indirect object pronouns are normally placed in front of the verb, but **loro** (often replaced by **gli** in modern Italian) always comes after the verb:
Le ho chiesto di spegnere la luce. I asked her to switch off the light.

With **dovere, potere, sapere, volere,** pronouns can be placed in front of the verb or after the infinitive:
Te lo posso mandare / Posso mandartelo. I can send it to you.

Emphatic pronouns are used with a preposition.
* for emphasis: **Questo regalo è per te.** This present is for you.
* when the verb has two or more direct or indirect objects:
Chiederò a lei non a lui. I shall ask her not him.
* as the second part of a comparison:
Sei più alto di me. You are taller than me.

Si is a reflexive pronoun meaning 'himself/herself/themselves' etc, but also 'one'. **Non si sa mai.** One never knows.

Ci to it/this/that, about it/this/that; here/there:
Pensaci! Think about it!

Ne 'of/about him/her/them/this; from here/there'.
Cosa ne pensate? What do you think about this?

When two pronouns are used, the indirect comes before the direct, or before **ne**.

Try to use some pronouns in your work e.g.
C'è troppa carta nella casa. Dovrei riciclarla.

➜ Useful pages in *Amici*: 81, 87, 90, 220–221

4 Business, work and employment

Work experience/part-time jobs/product or service information

Sono studente/ssa	*I am a student*
Sono disoccupato/a	*I am unemployed*
Mio padre è ingegnere	*My father is an engineer*
Mia madre è dottoressa	*My mother is a doctor*
Lavoro in un albergo	*I work in a hotel*
Lavora in una banca	*He works in a bank*
Lavoro per una società che si chiama ...	*I work for a company called ...*
Lavoro come infermiera	*I work as a nurse*
Io ho lavorato nei mesi estivi in un ufficio	*I worked in an office in the summer months*
L'anno scorso ho lavorato come cameriere/a	*Last year I worked as a waiter/ waitress*
Durante l'estate ho lavorato in un ristorante	*During the summer I worked in a restaurant*
Ho fatto un corso di informatica	*I have done an ICT course*
Mi piacerebbe viaggiare	*I would like to travel*
Mi piacerebbe tanto lavorare presso ...	*I'd very much like to work at ...*
Vorrei andare in Australia	*I'd like to go to Australia*
Vorrei diventare autista	*I'd like to be a driver*
Vorrei diventare giornalista	*I'd like to be a journalist*
Vorrei lavorare a tempo pieno	*I'd like to work full time*
Vorrei lavorare con gli animali	*I'd like to work with animals.*
Vorrei lavorare con i computer	*I'd like to work with computers*
Vorrei lavorare in un albergo / ristorante	*I'd like to work in a hotel / restaurant*
Vorrei studiare scienze all'università	*I would like to study science at university*
Desidero vivere in Italia	*I would like to live in Italy*
Ho intenzione di lavorare come traduttore/traduttrice	*I intend to work as a translator*
Ho un'ottima conoscenza dell'inglese scritto	*I have excellent written English*
Ho un'ottima conoscenza di Internet	*I have an excellent knowledge of the Internet*
Lavoro volentieri in un team	*I like to work in a team*
Spero di fare l'interprete	*I hope to be an interpreter*
Vorrei migliorare la mia conoscenza dell'italiano	*I would like to improve my Italian*

➜ Useful pages in *Amici*: 110–115, 168, 195

Advantages and disadvantages of different jobs

Mi piace il lavoro	*I like the job*
Mi piace tantissimo il mio lavoro	*I really like my job*
Il lavoro è interessante	*The job is interesting*
Non è un lavoro noioso	*It's not a boring job*
Comincio alle … Finisco alle …	*I start at … I finish at …*
L'orario è flessibile	*The hours are flexible*
Non devo lavorare il sabato	*I don't have to work on Saturdays*
Viaggio spesso	*I often travel*
Mi piace visitare altri Paesi	*I like to visit other countries*
Mi piace lavorare con i giovani	*I like working with young people*
Mi piaceva soprattutto incontrare i turisti	*Above all I liked meeting the tourists*
Alcuni turisti erano molto simpatici	*Some tourists were very nice*
Mi hanno pagato bene	*They paid me well*
Mi piaceva molto il lavoro	*I really liked the job*
Mi piacerebbe diventare sia attore che cantante rock	*I'd like to be an actor or a rock singer*
Mi piacerebbe diventare un giocatore di basket	*I'd like to become a basketball player*
Le piace il suo lavoro Gli piace il suo lavoro	*She likes her job* *He likes his job*

Il mio lavoro ha degli svantaggi	*My job has disadvantages*
È un lavoro duro	*It's a hard job*
Devo lavorare spesso a casa la sera	*I often have to work at home in the evening*
Questo è un vero svantaggio	*This is a real disadvantage*
Le ore lavorative sono lunghe	*The working hours are long*
Il lavoro è faticoso	*The job is tiring*
La paga è troppo bassa.	*The pay is too low*
Alcuni colleghi sono piuttosto antipatici	*Some colleagues are not very nice*
Non vado d'accordo con …	*I do not get on with …*
Non gli piace il suo lavoro Non le piace il suo lavoro	*He does not like his job* *She does not like her job*

➔ Useful pages in *Amici*: 112–115, 168, 195

1 Out and about

1.1 Visitor information

1. ☐☐ Read about Luisella's favourite town. (**F**)

> **Qual è la città italiana più bella che abbiate mai visitato?**
> La più bella che ho visitato ... allora sono belle Firenze, Venezia, Siena ma, secondo me, nessuna batte Roma!
> Quest'estate sono andata con i miei genitori a Roma. Abbiamo dormito nella nostra vecchia casa. I primi giorni abbiamo visitato il centro storico, poi siamo andati a salutare alcuni amici e per tutto il resto del tempo siamo stati al mare ad Ostia e abbiamo fatto compere. Verso la fine di luglio siamo stati una settimana a Tivoli da alcuni parenti. Sono stata davvero felice perché sono anche riuscita a passare qualche giorno con le mie vecchie compagne di scuola che non vedevo da tanto tempo. **Luisella**

Write the correct letter in the boxes.

(a) Luisella's favourite city is ...
  A Venice.   B Florence.   C Rome. ☐

(b) She went to Rome with her ...
  A relatives.   B parents.   C friends. ☐

(c) They visited the old part of the city ...
  A first.   B on the second last day.   C on the last day. ☐

(d) They went to Tivoli in ...   A June.   B January.   C July. ☐

(e) Luisella saw her old school friends for ...
  A a few days.   B one day.   C a month. ☐

(f) She last saw these school friends ...
  A a week ago.   B a few days ago.   C a long time ago. ☐

2. ◯ Listen to Luca talking about his holiday (CD track 2). Complete the grid. (**F**)

(a)	Luca visited	
(b)	with	
(c)	He left on	
(d)	The holiday lasted	
(e)	They travelled by	
(f)	He thought the holiday was	

3. 📖 Read Antonella's e-mail about a trip to Florence. (**F/H**)

> Ciao a tutti, bellissimi i miei tre giorni a Firenze. Due notti passate nella pensione di Elisabetta ed Antonio, simpaticissimi e molto disponibili. Sono arrivata da Genova all'una e mezza e, dopo aver posato la valigia in camera, Antonio mi ha dato una cartina di Firenze. Quindi già nel pomeriggio ho fatto una bella camminata visitando la chiesa di Santa Maria Novella, Palazzo Strozzi e Piazza Della Signoria. Il giorno dopo ho visitato ancora una volta Piazza della Signoria, gli Uffizi, Ponte Vecchio e Palazzo Pitti. L'ultimo giorno sono andato al Duomo e ho fatto un'altra visitina a Piazza Della Signoria. Sono rimasta stupefatta dalle meravigliose opere d'arte e dal gran numero di turisti presenti, soprattutto giapponesi. Ho apprezzato molto le vie del centro storico e le piccole botteghe. Non vi dico quante foto ho scattato! **_Antonella_**

According to Antonella's e-mail which of the following statements are: **T** (true), **F** (false), **?** (not in the text)?

(a) Antonella spent less than a week in Florence. ☐

(b) Elisabetta and Antonio were not very helpful. ☐

(c) Antonella took a taxi to the hotel. ☐

(d) She bought a map of Florence. ☐

(e) The first afternoon she went around on foot. ☐

(f) She visited Piazza della Signoria more than once. ☐

(g) There were lots of American tourists in Florence. ☐

(h) Unfortunately Antonella didn't take many photos. ☐

4. 🎧 Listen to the dialogue about Roberto's parents' holiday (CD track 3) and write the correct letter in the box. (**H**)

(a) Roberto's parents went to Boston ... ☐
  A for family reasons.   B on a business trip.   C to live.

(b) Roberto's brother is ... ☐
  A at university.   B looking for a job.   C working.

(c) Roberto's parents remained in Boston ... ☐
  A a month.   B two weeks.   C permanently.

(d) The parents' reaction to the States was ... ☐
  A negative.   B positive.   C positive and negative.

5. 🎧 Listen to Daniela talking about her trip (CD track 4) and complete the table. (**H**)

(a)	Time of arrival	
(b)	Season	
(c)	Mode of transport from airport	
(d)	Type of accommodation	
(e)	Animals living on Phillip Island	
(f)	Distance of island from city	

1.2 Basic weather

1. 🎧 Listen to these people talking about what the weather was like during their holidays (CD track 5). Match the town with the weather conditions and put the correct letter in the box. **(F)**

(a)	Barcelona	
(b)	Chicago	
(c)	Cortina	
(d)	Edinburgh	
(e)	London	
(f)	Madrid	
(g)	Manchester	
(h)	Marseille	
(i)	Milan	

2. ☐☐ Read the weather forecast for the coming week. **(H)**

SABATO tempo instabile al Centro Sud, piogge e frequenti temporali al Sud su Sicilia, Calabria, e a Sud della Sardegna.

DOMENICA Attenzione alla nebbia lungo il Po, tra Lombardia ed Emilia.

LUNEDI ancora instabile al Sud, specie su Puglia, Calabria. Nebbia nelle prime ore del mattino sulla Valpadana.

MARTEDI temporali su Calabria, piogge su Liguria. Neve sulle Alpi.

MERCOLEDI maltempo con temporali al Nordest. Neve a 900m sul Nord Appennino

GIOVEDI migliora al Nord, sole in Liguria, ma rovesci sul Sud.

VENERDI attenzione nuova perturbazione da Nord, di nuovo maltempo al Centro Sud e Nordest, a seguire temperature in ribasso.

On which day might you find ...

(a) rain in Liguria?

(b) fog around the River Po?

(c) storms in Sicily?

(d) better weather in the North than the South?

(e) snow in the Apennines?

1.3 Local amenities

1. 🎧 Listen to the description of Lido di Jesolo (CD track 6). Complete the missing information by selecting the answer from the box. **(F)**

(a) There are about _____ hotels and guest houses.

(b) There are _____ villas and apartments.

(c) There are _____ swimming pools.

(d) The swimming pools are very near the
_____ .

(e) They are not far from the Venetian
_____ .

(f) The season starts in _____ .

beach	May	45000	120	12000	450	town centre
June	countryside	September		4500	first	

2. 📖 Read these comments about three Italian towns and answer the questions. Write **B** (Beatrice), **C** (Carla), or **A** (Aldo) in the box. **(F/H)**

Io sono di ROMA ... e amo la mia città, qualcuno potrebbe dire che è chiassosa, piena di turisti, caotica ... ma io la amo!! ... Quando passo per il centro storico respiro e dico ... ma come sono fortunata! i monumenti, le fontane, le piazze, e gli abitanti ... cordiali, gentili ... e poi sono felice di tutti i punti di ritrovo per giovani … teatri, cinema, scuole, possibilità di fare qualsiasi cosa ... e poi io non me ne andrei mai da questa città perché è magica ... **Beatrice**

Io vivo a Torino e la amo. Abbastanza pulita, colorata, piena di cultura, feste, incontri, negozi particolari. Ogni giorno scopro un angolo nuovo. Negozi dove anche gli animali sono accolti calorosamente ... Locali dove puoi bere un aperitivo mentre lavi la roba ... Negozi aperti 24 ore su 24 ... Attività di ogni tipo per i giovani ... Concerti ... Teatro. Viva Torino! **Aldo**

Ciao, io trovo Pisa una città bellissima, io ci studio, frequento la facoltà di Giurisprudenza ma comunque vivo a Torre del Lago Puccini. Da quando ho iniziato a studiare qui, voglio rimanerci sempre, anche quando l'università è chiusa e spesso infatti ci sono tornata con il mio ragazzo e ci siamo seduti in riva all'Arno ad ammirare il paesaggio e gli edifici storici riflessi sull'acqua. È una città intellettuale e carica di arte, mi piace moltissimo! Baci, **Carla**

Who ...

(a) has sat by the river and admired the landscape? ☐

(b) says there are fountains in the town? ☐

(c) says their town is clean? ☐

(d) studies Law in Pisa? ☐

(e) says dogs are welcome in some shops? ☐

(f) never wants to leave the town? ☐

(g) says you can have a drink while doing your washing? ☐

1.4 Accommodation

1. 🎧 Listen to the dialogue at the hotel (CD track 7) and fill in the details. **(F)**

(a)	Number of nights customer wants to stay?	
(b)	Type of rooms needed?	
(c)	Bath or shower?	
(d)	Price?	
(e)	Is there a lift?	
(f)	What time is breakfast?	

2. ▭ Read these descriptions of two hotels. **(H)**

A Qui puoi trovare tranquillità, divertimenti per piccoli e grandi, svago e sport. Per una passeggiata in pineta e nel parco, biciclette gratuite per i nostri clienti. Mare tranquillo e sicuro: spiaggia attrezzatissima e indicata per grandi e piccoli ospiti, tennis, maneggio, campi da calcetto, deltaplani, golf, canotaggio, ecc.

Nei dintorni: Ravenna con i mosaici, Faenza con la ceramica, San Marino, Venezia, Ferrara.

B L'albergo è situato di fronte al mare, in zona tranquilla, al margine di una bellissima pineta che costeggia il litorale. Inoltre offre tutti i confort: camere con TV e telefono; bagni rinnovati con phon. Servizio fax, cassaforte, parcheggio auto. Sala colazione a buffet, servizio bar, cabina alla spiaggia, sala ristorante climatizzata. Servizio biciclette gratuito.

Which hotel would you recommend to these people?
Write **A**, **B** or **A+B**.

(a)	Anna likes peace and quiet.	
(b)	Caterina loves horse riding.	
(c)	Gianni loves playing five-a-side.	
(d)	Sara needs a hairdryer in the bathroom!	
(e)	Stefano insists on a safe in the room.	
(f)	Martino loves hang gliding.	
(g)	Martina wants to get changed on the beach.	
(h)	Angela wants to visit Venice.	
(i)	Paolo loves cycling.	

3. Listen to this dialogue at a campsite (CD track 8) and complete the information. **(F)**

(a)	Number of tents?	
(b)	Number of nights?	
(c)	Type of transport?	
(d)	Price?	
(f)	What sport does the man play?	

4. Listen to someone talking about their home (CD track 9) and answer the following questions. **(H)**

(a) What kind of house is being described and where is it located?

(b) When is it possible to take advantage of the garden and for what occasion?

(c) How many bathrooms are there and where are they?

(d) What is another outside attraction of the house?

(e) What is the main disadvantage of living in this area and why?

5. Read about a campsite. **(H)**

Il campeggio è situato in una valle. La sua capacità ricettiva è di 80 posti, dotato di ampie tende da 2 a 4 letti. I servizi comprendono 3 docce con acqua calda, 6 servizi e una serie di lavabi. Tutto rinnovato nella scorsa stagione. La cucina è dotata delle più moderne attrezzature ed i pasti vengono serviti in una nuova ed ampia tenda soggiorno direttamente collegata con la tenda bar.

Ci sono infinite possibilità di escursioni alpinistiche ... trekking, canoa, rafting, pesca alla trota, raccolta di funghi e più di 200 Km. di sentieri per mountain bike.

Which of the following statements are: **T** (true), **F** (false), **?** (not in the text)?

(a) The campsite is situated by the sea. ☐

(b) The campsite tents can sleep 2–4 people. ☐

(c) There is no hot water. ☐

(d) There is a tent for live music. ☐

(e) You can go mushroom picking. ☐

1.5 Public transport

1. ⌒ Listen to the dialogues (CD track 10) and fill in the grid. **(F/H)**

	Type of ticket	Destination	Price	Departs at	Platform number
(a)					
(b)					
(c)					

2. ☐☐ Read the following comments. **(H)**

Write **G** (Graziano), **S** (Stefania), or **N** (Nicolò) in the box.

La colpa è soprattutto del traffico. Ci sono persone che non escono mai senz'auto. Penso che si debbano usare carburanti meno nocivi.

Graziano

L'inquinamento atmosferico ha molte cause, ad esempio il traffico veicolare, le emissioni delle industrie. Dobbiamo riscoprire il treno, il bus, la bicicletta! È essenziale che siano potenziati i mezzi pubblici e si incoraggi un utilizzo diverso dell'automobile.

Stefania

Le "domeniche del pedone" hanno insegnato alla gente a ritrovarsi, andare a piedi, fare un giro in bicicletta con gli amici.

Nicolò

(a)	Who thinks we should start to use trains, buses and bicycles more?	
(b)	Who thinks there are people who cannot live without their car?	
(c)	Who thinks cars and industry are responsible for pollution?	
(d)	Who thinks that new initiatives like car-free Sundays have helped?	

1.6 Directions

1. ◯ Listen to the directions (CD track 11), then fill in the gaps in the following sentences. **(F/H)**

(a) To get to the park, _____ the square,
go _____ and take the first street on the
_____ . The park is at the bottom of
that street.

(b) Go straight on to the second set of
_____ , turn
_____ and the car park is on the right,
behind the supermarket.

(c) It's not far. It is five minutes _____ .
Go straight on and take the _____
street on your right and the hotel is on the right,
_____ the cinema.

(d) Go straight on to the _____ , then turn
left and it's there on the left. It's _____
a pizzeria.

2. ▢▢ Read the following directions to a hotel. **(F)**

COME ARRIVARE ALL'ALBERGO PANORAMIC

L'Albergo Panoramic dista meno di 2 km dalla Stazione Centrale ed è facilmente raggiungibile sia in autobus sia in automobile.

AUTOBUS: linea n°18 consente di raggiungere l'albergo da diversi punti della città, fra cui il centro storico e la stazione. La frequenza giornaliera dalle ore 7.00 alle ore 20.00 è di circa 10–15 minuti dal lunedì al sabato, ogni 20–30 minuti la domenica e i festivi.

AUTOMOBILE:
Dalla Tangenziale: uscita n°12 della Tangenziale. Ai semafori ubicati in fondo alle rampe di uscita, si trovano le indicazioni stradali per l'Albergo Panoramic.
Dalla Stazione Centrale: percorrere via Cavour in direzione Porta Mascherate, girare a sinistra in via Matteotti. All'incrocio con via XX Settembre girare a sinistra. Proseguire fino ad incontrare via Franco Viti e girare a sinistra. L'albergo si trova al numero 40. L'albergo dispone di un ampio parcheggio interno, gratuito.

Which of the following statements are: **T** (true), **F** (false),
? (not in the text)?

(a) The hotel is less than 2 kilometres from the station. ▢

(b) The number 18 bus runs every 20–30 minutes on a Monday. ▢

(c) You need to drive 30 miles along the ring road. ▢

(d) The address of the hotel is 40 Via Franco Viti. ▢

(e) You have to pay 40 euros to park in the car park. ▢

2 Customer service and transactions

2.1 Cafés and restaurants

1. 🎧 Listen to what the man orders in a restaurant (CD track 12). **(F/H)**

   Put a ✗ next to the **four correct** items.

   He orders ...

(a)	a starter.	
(b)	soup.	
(c)	steak.	
(d)	chips and a mixed salad.	
(e)	a beer.	
(f)	half a litre of white wine.	
(g)	a bottle of still mineral water.	
(h)	a strawberry ice cream.	

2. 📖 In a restaurant you notice a good choice of spaghetti! **(F)**

   > **Una bella spaghettata!**
   >
   > Spaghetti al burro
   > Spaghetti al tonno
   > Spaghetti al salmone
   > Spaghetti al pomodoro fresco
   > Spaghetti al limone
   > Spaghetti ai formaggi

   What sort of spaghetti can you order? Put a ✗ in the four correct boxes.

A	B	C	D	E	F	G	H
prawns	tuna	mushroom	butter	cheese	mussels	tomato	squid

3. 📖 Read about Pizzafest and answer the questions below. **(H)**

   (a) How is Pizzafest described?

   (b) How many days does Pizzafest last?

   (c) Give two drinks you might be offered at Pizzafest.

   > Torna l'appuntamento con Pizzafest, la più importante festa dedicata alla pizza napoletana. Offre al suo vasto pubblico undici giorni interamente dedicati al piatto per eccellenza della tradizione napoletana. Il tutto offerto al pubblico con la solita formula pizza, birra, limoncello, caffè e tanto, tanto divertimento!

2.2 Shops

1. Marco goes shopping. Listen to the dialogue (CD track 13) and complete the table. **(F)**

(a)	Article of clothing	
(b)	Measurement	
(c)	Preferred colour	
(d)	Colour finally chosen	
(e)	Cost	€

2. Listen to the following extract about the Internet (CD track 14) and complete the sentences. **(F/H)**

   (a) Shopping online is very _____ especially in the _____ .

   (b) Now there is also an increase of _____ in Europe.

   (c) The percentage of people shopping online in Italy is _____ whereas in _____ it is 47%.

   (d) In the UK the figure is _____ and in _____ 65%.

   (e) The number of Internet users is predicted to go from 150 to _____ million.

3. Read these opinions about fashion and match the statements to the people. Write **S** (Silvana), **B** (Barbara), **L** (Leonardo) or **E** (Elvina). **(H)**

Dipende da come mi sento ... in genere mi vesto glam, ma sempre con qualche tocco di stravaganza. **Silvana**

Se c'è qualcosa che mi piace la prendo ... non vado certo a spendere dei milioni per delle cose che non mi piacciono o che non mi stanno bene!! **Barbara**

Conosco le ultime tendenze e so cosa propone la moda ... ma non mi faccio influenzare molto! **Leonardo**

Mi piace fare shopping, magari con qualche amica. Mi piace girare per negozi, provarmi quello che mi piace e comperare tutto ciò che soddisfi il mio ego. L'importante è che sia sempre qualcosa di elegante. **Elvina**

   (a) How I dress depends on how I feel. ☐

   (b) I enjoy going around the shops. ☐

   (c) I am not easily influenced by fashion. ☐

   (d) I have to have something that is really elegant. ☐

   (e) I certainly don't spend lots of money buying clothes that don't suit me. ☐

2.2 Shops *continued*

4. 📖 Where would you go to buy the following food? Put the correct letter in the box. **(F)**

(a)	I need some bread	
(b)	I need some meat	
(c)	I need some fruit	
(d)	I need an ice cream	

A GELATERIA
B LIBRERIA
C PANIFICIO
D FARMACIA
E FIORAIO
F FRUTTIVENDOLO
H MACELLERIA

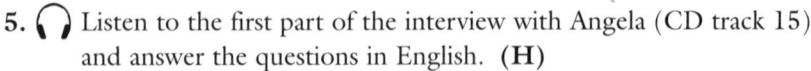

5. 🎧 Listen to the first part of the interview with Angela (CD track 15) and answer the questions in English. **(H)**

(a) How long has Angela worked in the shop and who does she work with?

(b) Has the arrival of the shopping centres affected the shop? Justify your answer.

(c) What **three** factors have contributed to the success of the supermarkets?

(d) What are the positive and negative outcomes of the supermarkets' success? Mention **three** points.

6. 🎧 Listen to the remainder of the interview (CD track 16) and complete the sentences. **(H)**

(a) One of the advantages small shops have over supermarkets is that they can offer more _____ .

(b) Many of their customers are also _____ .

(c) The supermarket is very _____ .

(d) Most of the customers are in the _____ age bracket and they live _____ .

2.3 Dealing with problems

1. ◯ Listen and choose the ending that completes each sentence (CD track 17). Put the letter in the correct box. **(F)**

(a)	This person is asking for the ...	
(b)	The coffee is ...	
(c)	This person did not order ...	
(d)	There's a mistake in the ...	
(e)	This person needs a ...	
(f)	This person's glass is ...	

A cheese.
B fork.
C menu.
D dirty.
E spoon
F cold.
G bill.
H hot.
I wet.

2. ◯ Listen to Daniela's conversation in a clothes shop (CD track 18) and answer the questions. **(F/H)**

(a) When did she buy the jeans?

(b) What is the problem?

(c) What does the assistant offer?

(d) Why can Daniela not have her money back?

(e) What does Daniela agree to in the end?

3. ▢▢ Read the problem and the two replies. **(H)**

Domanda	Risposte
Mia moglie mi ha regalato un cellulare che non mi piace. Io adesso vorrei passare al negozio e farmi ridare i soldi. Il negoziante è obbligato per legge a ridarmi i soldi? Oppure no? **Carlo**	Più facile cambiare la moglie! **Aldo**
	Se è un regalo e se è ancora integro nella scatola non vedo perché il negoziante non dovrebbe cambiarlo con un altro. **Lina**

Put a ✗ in the boxes next to the **four correct** statements.

(a)	Carlo's wife gave him a present he doesn't like.	
(b)	He wants her to take it back to the shop.	
(c)	He wants a cash refund.	
(d)	Aldo says it would be easier to change the wife.	
(e)	Lina says he would need the original receipt.	
(f)	Lina can't see why he would not be able to exchange the gift.	

3 Personal information

3.1 General interests

1. ◯ Listen to five people saying what they enjoy doing (CD track 19) and complete the table with the correct letter. **(F)**

Person	Interest
1	
2	
3	
4	
5	

2. ☐☐ Read what Stefania, Flavio and Marco have to say about their free time. **(F)**

Come passatempi vado su internet per chattare e a volte leggo ma non sono per niente sportivo. A me piace uscire con gli amici per non stare con i miei genitori perché stare con loro è noioso! Andiamo spesso al cinema, non importa quale film danno. **Flavio**

Nel mio tempo libero faccio un po' di tutto: pratico diversi sport, guardo la tv, vado in giro con i miei amici, ascolto musica e suono la chitarra o il pianoforte. A tutti questi hobby dedico molto tempo. **Stefania**

Io dedico poco tempo libero allo sport perché di solito ho troppi compiti. L'unico sport che mi piace è il calcio ma gioco raramente. La mia passione è il cinema ma vado a vedere solo i film di avventura, dell'orrore o di fantascienza. **Marco**

Which of the following people might get on well with **S** (Stefania), **F** (Flavio) or **M** (Marco)?

(a) Ed does not like sports much, but loves watching all sorts of films. ☐

(b) Sarah likes reading and chatting on the Internet. ☐

(c) Antony loves football and science fiction films. ☐

(d) Lyndsey loves playing lots of different sports. ☐

(e) David prefers going out with his friends to spending time with his parents. ☐

3. Listen to five people expressing their opinions (CD track 20). Put a ✗ in the correct box. **(F)**

Person	Positive	Negative	Positive + Negative
1			
2			
3			
4			
5			

4. Read Valeria's *MySpace* information. **(F/H)**

> **myspace**　　　　　　　　**Valeria**
>
> **Adoro interagire con culture diverse dalla mia, così come parlare e imparare lingue straniere. Non sempre è possibile viaggiare e tastare direttamente nuove terre, perciò m'interesso di fotografia d'autore che mi permette di viaggiare con la fantasia e vedere altri mondi indirettamente. Tra i miei fotografi preferiti vi sono: Olivier Föllmi, Steve McCurry e Elliott Erwitt. Nel mio tempo libero mi dedico al disegno, al déco, senza tralasciare la visione di qualche film, la lettura e lo sport (volleyball e nuoto).**　　　　*Valeria*

Put a ✗ in the boxes next to the **four correct** statements.

(a)	Valeria loves foreign languages.	
(b)	She is always travelling around the world.	
(c)	She is interested in photography.	
(d)	She can't stand volleyball.	
(e)	She loves reading.	
(f)	She enjoys swimming.	
(g)	She rarely goes to the cinema.	

5. Listen to these dialogues about films (CD track 21) and answer the questions in English. **(H)**

Dialogue 1 (a) What was the film that Ernestina saw about?

(b) What effect did the film have on her and why was this such a good thing?

Dialogue 2 (a) What was **good** about the film that Alberto saw?

(b) Mention **two** things he disliked about the film.

Dialogue 3 (a) What was Marina's reason for going to see the film 'Camera con vista'?

(b) Why would Marina not be able to comment on the film?

3.2 Leisure activities

1. 🎧 Listen to what Daniela's mother does during the week (CD track 22) and complete the missing information in the grid. **(F/H)**

	When	Activity	Where	With
(a)	Tuesday evening			
(b)	Wednesday evening			
(c)	Thursday evening			
(d)	Friday morning			
(e)	Friday evening			
(f)	Saturday evening			

2. ☐☐ Read what Cinzia and Lorenzo do in their free time. **(H)**

Nel mio tempo libero faccio un po' di tutto: pratico sport (ginnastica), guardo la tv, vado in giro con i miei amici, ascolto musica, vado su internet per chattare e a volte leggo. A tutti questi hobby dedico molto tempo, soprattutto alla ginnastica che pratico tre volte alla settimana per due ore e mezza al giorno. Lo sport permette molta socialità perché non è praticato singolarmente ma a gruppi di più persone. Questo aspetto secondo me è molto positivo e secondo me ho bisogno di avere qualche amico che mi faccia compagnia. Ho scelto io lo sport che pratico, e non lo faccio solo per stare con i miei amici, ma anche per una mia passione personale.
Cinzia

Di solito uso il mio tempo libero per stare con gli amici; mi diverto a stare con loro perché imparo a condividere le mie e le loro esperienze e a rispettare il prossimo. Inoltre chiacchieriamo e ci scambiamo confidenze. Comunque io il tempo libero lo uso anche per leggere, guardare la tv, ascoltare la musica o praticare dello sport, ma la cosa che mi piace di più resta sempre l'amicizia dei miei amici.
Lorenzo

Answer **C** (Cinzia), **L** (Lorenzo) or **C+L** (Cinzia + Lorenzo).

(a) Who enjoys watching television? ☐

(b) Who does gymnastics three times a week? ☐

(c) Who enjoys visiting chat rooms? ☐

(d) Who enjoys the company of friends? ☐

(e) Who has learned to share experiences? ☐

3. ▢▢ Read this chat page about going to the gym.

	Chi va in palestra? **Quante volte a settimana?** **Da quanto tempo?**
chloe	Vado due volte alla settimana da circa un anno e mezzo.
elio	Prima ci andavo due giorni sí, tre giorni no ... Poi da quando ho finito la scuola a giugno ho iniziato ad andarci quasi tutti i giorni ... ho smesso a metà luglio perché sono andato in vacanza e ho ricominciato da lunedì ... per ora ci vado spesso poi quando inizia la scuola vedrò.
maia	Ci andavo l'anno scorso, seguivo il corso di autodifesa e facevo gli attrezzi. Ci andavo dalle 8 in poi di sera fino alle 10 (poi chiude), MI AMMAZZAVO!!! dopo un po' mi annoiavo.
lino	Io voglio andarci assolutamente, ma non trovo tempo.
guido	Ora come ora ci vado tutti i giorni, non ho nulla da fare di particolarmente intenso ... Con l'università è più duro perché torno sempre esausto ... però di solito facevo dalle 7 alle 8,30 ... Nel periodo degli esami la faccio in casa, non ho tempo!
pia	Quest'anno volevo iscrivermi, ma prima devo vedere se riesco ad organizzarmi tra scuola, lavoro e volontariato.

Complete these sentences with the correct name. **(H)**

(a) _____ has been going to the gym for a year and a half.

(b) _____ stopped going in July.

(c) _____ has to fit it in with school and voluntary work.

(d) _____ started to get bored after a while.

(e) _____ wants to go but can't find the time.

(f) _____ is going every day.

(g) _____ went to self-defence classes.

3.3 Family and friends

1. ◯ Listen to Lorenzo (CD track 23) and complete the table. **(F)**

(a)	Girlfriend's name	
(b)	Age	
(c)	Number of brothers and sisters	
(d)	Place of birth	
(e)	Character	

2. ⬚ Read about these students' family and friends. **(F/H)**

Mi chiamo **Naima**, sono nata a Venezia. Ho sedici anni. Ho una sorella che si chiama Amanda. Mio padre si chiama Daniele ed è un ingegnere. Sono studentessa al liceo a Mestre. I miei hobby sono la chitarra e il nuoto. Le mie amiche sono Giulia e Cecilia, siamo molto amiche da un anno. Non mi piace molto la scuola!

Mi chiamo **Claudia**, ho quindici anni. Abito a Ginevra. Sono italiana. Ho un fratello, Massimo, e una sorella, Sonia. Hanno 22 e 26 anni. Mia sorella è sposata e ha tre figli, Cassandra, Naomi e Martino. Suo marito si chiama Aldo. I miei genitori si chiamano Maria e Mario. Mia madre è casalinga e mio padre è albergatore. Non ho animali. Sono studentessa. I miei migliori amici sono Carolina, Catia e Linda.

Mi chiamo **Domenico**. Ho 15 anni. Sono nato a Firenze il 29 ottobre 1985. Abito a Fiesole. La famiglia di mio padre vive a Venezia e Parma; la famiglia di mia madre è di Ginevra. Ho un fratello, si chiama Franco, i miei genitori si chiamano Maurizio e Chantal. Mio padre è italiano e mia madre è svizzera. Non ho sorelle.

Answer these questions in English:

(a) What is Naima's sister called?

(b) What is Naima's father's job?

(c) How long has Naima been friends with Giulia?

(d) How many children has Claudia's sister got?

(e) What does Claudia's father do for a living?

(f) How many animals does Claudia have?

(g) What nationality is Domenico's father?

(h) What nationality is Domenico's mother?

3. Listen to the dialogues (CD track 24) and choose a word from the list that best describes each person. Write the correct letter in the table. (**H**)

	Person	Letter
(a)	Stefano	
(b)	Germana	
(c)	Sonia	
(d)	Marinella	
(e)	Roberto	
(f)	Filippo	

A pessimist
B egotistical
C honest
D spoilt
E inquisitive
F optimist
G ambitious
H lazy
I perfectionist

4. Read about Matteo's and Francesca's families. (**F/H**)

Matteo

Fratelli! Che sarebbe la mia famiglia senza di loro? Io sono il mezzano, nel senso che ho un fratello più grande e una sorella più piccola e anche se qualche volta litighiamo, io li amo da morire!

Francesca

Sì sono d'accordo ... è stupendo avere un fratello o una sorella anche perché per tutta la vita avremo una persona su cui poter contare ... sì, sono davvero contenta di non essere figlia unica, anche perché con un fratello e una sorella impari moltissimo, impari a non essere egoista, ma a condividere, impari ad essere una persona migliore ...

Answer the following questions. Write **M** (Matteo), **F** (Francesca), **M+F** (Matteo and Francesca) or **N** (neither).

(a) Who is happy not to be an only child? ☐

(b) Who has a brother and a sister? ☐

(c) Who quarrels all the time? ☐

(d) Who has a younger sister? ☐

(e) Who adopts a negative attitude to their brother or sister? ☐

(f) Who will learn not to be selfish? ☐

3.4 Lifestyle (healthy eating and exercise)

1. ▢▢ Read the comments about people's lifestyles. **(F)**

Mangiare sano, vivere meglio!

Antonio: mangio sempre prodotti biologici, frutta e verdura a volontà, pasta, riso, insalata e poca carne.

Elena: cerco di mangiare un po' di frutta e verdura ogni giorno perché so che mi fa bene ma poi mi piacciono tanto le patatine, il cioccolato, gli hamburger ...

Giorgio: non seguo una dieta sana e non pratico nessuno sport ma sono contento lo stesso.

Clara: vado sempre a scuola a piedi perché mi piace tanto camminare. Durante l'intervallo mangio una mela o una banana, mai le caramelle o le patatine.

Enrico: non pratico nessuno sport da tanti anni e sono diventato veramente pigro perché vado dappertutto in macchina. Quanto alla dieta, mangio tutte le cose che per la salute non dovrei mangiare.

What is the attitude of these people to a healthy lifestyle? Write **P** (positive), **N** (negative) or **P+N** (positive and negative).

	Person	Letter
Example:	Antonio	*P*
(a)	Elena	
(b)	Giorgio	
(c)	Clara	
(d)	Enrico	

2. 🎧 Listen to this information about Cristina (CD track 25). Complete the table. **(H)**

Example:	Place of work	*Office*
(a)	**Two** after-work activities	
(b)	How she learned about diet	
(c)	Her everyday diet	
(d)	Main meal preference	

3. ◯ Listen to Luisa's conversation with her friend (CD track 26) and answer the following questions. (H)

(a) What was Luisa's attitude to sport at school?
(b) Who does she thank for her recent interest in sport and why?
(c) What **two** activities does she now do and how often?
(d) What **two** things did she use to eat for breakfast?
(e) What does she regularly drink for breakfast?
(f) How has her attitude to food and drink changed?

4. ▢▢ Giovanni talks about his lifestyle. (F/H)

Come ti tieni in forma?

Sono Giovanni e per tenermi in forma vado in palestra due o tre volte alla settimana, e pratico molto sport, in particolare gli sport acquatici come la vela, la pesca e faccio sub. Amo stare all'aria aperta e le mie attività preferite sono lo sci, fare footing e andare in bici. Durante il giorno conduco una vita sedentaria perché lavoro in ufficio e per la maggior parte del tempo sono seduto davanti al computer. Per fortuna con tutto lo sport che faccio non ho mai avuto problemi di sovrappeso.

Put a ✗ in the boxes next to the **four correct** statements.

(a)	He goes to the gym at least twice a week.	
(b)	He always goes to the gym on Fridays.	
(c)	He is not very keen on fishing.	
(d)	He likes various outdoor activities.	
(e)	He works in an office.	
(f)	He works flexi-time.	
(g)	His job involves a lot of standing around.	
(h)	He has never had weight problems.	

4 Future plans, education and work

4.1 Basic language of the internet

1. ▢ Read this advice given to parents. **(F)**

Genitori! È importante ...

- non mettere un computer nella stanza del bambino.
- stabilire regole precise su come utilizzare Internet.
- conoscere gli amici on-line dei figli.
- installare un software che memorizzi i siti visitati dal bambino.
- usare software di protezione.
- tenere i bambini lontani dalle chat-room.
- far capire ai propri figli di non dare alcuna informazione personale (indirizzo, scuola frequentata ...).

Put a **✗** in the boxes next to the **four correct** statements.

It is important that parents ...

(a)	do not put a computer in a child's room	
(b)	establish clear rules as to how the Internet should be used	
(c)	only allow their children to use the Internet with reliable friends	
(d)	get to know their children's on-line friends	
(e)	only allow restricted use of chatrooms	
(f)	ensure their children understand that they should not give out personal information	
(g)	ensure children give the school, not the home e-mail address	

2. 🎧 Listen to Daniela, Alessandra and Gianpaolo discussing chatrooms (CD track 27) and answer these questions in English. **(H)**

(a) According to Daniela, what are the main advantages of chatrooms?

(b) Apart from friends, who else can you communicate with?

(c) What does Alessandra say you might find?

(d) What is Gianpaolo's attitude to chatrooms and why?

3. ☐☐ Read this text about the Internet. **(F/H)**

> Internet, televisione telefonini … tutta la moderna tecnologia di oggi è usata per lavorare, per studiare e persino per trovare il compagno ideale. In un futuro non lontano, non sarà difficile incontrare qualche signora ottantenne seduta al bar sotto casa, che con un telefonino dell'ultima generazione, prenota un appuntamento dalla parrucchiera, o manda la lista della spesa al supermercato. Sarà anche possibile fare videotelefonate con i cellulari.

A	appointments at the hairdresser's.
B	shopping via their mobile phones.
C	at an Internet café.
D	to make video calls.
E	work and study.
F	to call your boss.
G	your ideal partner.
H	doctor's appointment by mobile.

Choose the correct ending from the box above to complete the following sentences.

(a)	Modern technology is used for …	
(b)	You can even find …	
(c)	80 year olds will soon be ordering their …	
(d)	They will also be able to make …	
(e)	You will be able to use your mobile …	

4. ☐☐ Read about the advantages and disadvantages of the computer and answer the questions in English. **(H)**

Vantaggi:
- ti permette di fare diversi tipi di operazioni che ti fanno risparmiare moltissimo tempo – invio di messaggi di testo, prenotazione di biglietti aerei o ferroviari on line, fare acquisti senza muoverti da casa.
- il telelavoro: è meno costoso lavorare da casa.
- la ricerca di qualsiasi tipo di informazione in modo facile e veloce – basta digitare poche parole chiave su google per trovare le previsioni del tempo, la distanza dell'albergo dall'aeroporto ecc.

Svantaggi:
- il costo e la capacità di utilizzarlo che non tutti hanno, in particolare gli anziani.
- i problemi di salute: per esempio alla schiena, agli occhi ecc.

(a) Why might a computer save you lots of time?

(b) What advantages does the computer have for the working person?

(c) What sort of useful research can you do on-line?

(d) Who might find the computer difficult and why?

(e) What health problems can the computer pose?

4.2 Simple job advertisements

1. ☐☐ Read the following job adverts and then match up the right person for the job. Write the correct letter in the boxes. **(F/H)**

A Cercasi commessa/o esperta/o part-time per negozio calzature in Sesto Fiorentino. Inviare curriculum con autorizzazione al trattamento dei dati personali.

B Cerchiamo per tutte le città italiane persone serie e motivate per aprire nuova redazione di un quotidiano on line a network nazionale.

C Lavoro da casa con Internet, indipendente ed autonomo, sia part-time che full-time, senza alcun obbligo di orari. Se pensi di essere una persona dinamica con: grande determinazione, ottime capacità relazionali, intraprendenza e volontà di lavorare in autonomia, allora la nostra attività online da casa potrebbe fare per te.

D Agenti rappresentanti per vendita olio e vino in tutta Italia ed estero.

E Studio legale con sede a Berlino (Germania) cerca giovane avvocato (ambosessi) con buone conoscenze della lingua tedesca/inglese. Ottime prospettive di carriera.

F Cerco cuoco per ristorante a pranzo e cena con esperienza lavorativa, veloce nella preparazione e organizzazione del servizio, serio, disponibile a effettuare servizi di catering in caso di necessità.

(a) John has done a high level wine tasting course and would like to work as a salesman abroad. ☐

(b) Mary studied journalism at university. She speaks Italian and is highly motivated. ☐

(c) Susan already works as a solicitor, is career-minded and speaks fluent French and German. ☐

(d) Mark is an experienced sales assistant. He has worked in several different shops and also had a job in Italy. ☐

(e) Julia would like to spend more time with her children and wants a job where she can work from home. ☐

2. 🎧 Listen to Daniela who is looking for work (CD track 28) and answer the following questions in English. **(H)**

(a) What is Daniela doing and where is she looking for the information?

(b) Where would she like to work and why?

(c) What is she unsure about and why?

(d) What does she need to do and why?

(e) What is her reaction to a job in a call centre?

4.3 Simple job applications and CV

1. ☐☐ Read this model curriculum vitae. **(F)**

Curriculum Vitae

Dati Anagrafici (Nome, Cognome; Nato a *** (**) il **/**/****; Residente in Via/Piazza ******; Cap Città; Tel *** :: Cel *** E-mail; Nazionalità)

Istruzione e Formazione 2008 – Laurea in ***** 110/110 - Università ***
2004 – Diploma Maturità Scientifica – Liceo ***** città

Esperienze Professionali 2006–2009 Azienda – posizione ecc.

Lingue Straniere INGLESE: padronanza della lingua inglese sia scritta che orale. TEDESCO: buona conoscenza della lingua tedesca. FRANCESE: conoscenza scolastica.

Conoscenze Informatiche *Microsoft Office* ecc.

Interessi Extraprofessionali (Elenca i viaggi, gli sport praticati, cinema, letture ecc.)

Progetti per il Futuro (Qui i tuoi progetti per il futuro ...)

Put a ✗ in the boxes next to the **four correct** statements.

Details you must give:

(a)	full personal details, including nationality	
(b)	date of degree and university details	
(c)	primary school information	
(d)	level of foreign language knowledge	
(e)	courses attended	
(f)	personal interest in the company	
(g)	other interests such as reading etc	

2. 🎧 Listen to Gianni and Gianpaolo talking about interviews (CD track 29). **(H)**

A	services the company offers.	B	long and short term goals
C	often the company is audited.	D	long the company has been in business.
E	quality assurance procedures.	F	on the Internet.
G	very important.	H	clear.

Choose the correct ending from the box above to complete the following sentences.

Gianpaolo ...

(a)	says every job interview is ...	
(b)	suggests finding out what ...	
(c)	suggests Gianni finds out how ...	
(d)	thinks Gianni should find out the company's ...	
(e)	suggests Gianni should do some research ...	

4.4 School and college

1. ☐☐ Read Marco's description of his school. **(F/H)**

> **La nostra aula** è al primo piano della scuola. È un'aula molto spaziosa che dà sui campi sportivi. Il mio banco è accanto alla finestra e quindi se la lezione è noiosa posso guardare quelli che giocano a calcio o a pallacanestro. Nell'aula ci sono parecchi scaffali dove ci sono libri e quaderni di alunni e maestri ma purtroppo non abbiamo computer.
>
> **La biblioteca** è spaziosa e luminosa. Si trova al piano terra, proprio davanti all'ingresso. Lungo le pareti ci sono gli scaffali con i libri ed in un angolo c'è la scrivania dove il bibliotecario segna al computer i libri che prendiamo in prestito. La parete davanti all'entrata è tutta a vetri e c'è la porta per uscire in giardino. In biblioteca c'è sempre silenzio e ci vado spesso a fare i miei compiti.
>
> **L'aula di informatica** si trova al secondo piano ed è abbastanza ampia e luminosa. Nell'aula computer, appena si entra a destra, ci sono quattro computer, a sinistra invece ce ne sono sei. Davanti alla porta c'è una lavagna ed accanto alla lavagna ci sono delle grandi finestre.

Put a **✗** in the boxes next to the **four correct** statements.

(a)	Marco's desk is next to the window.	
(b)	He plays football during the break.	
(c)	There is no space for pupils' books in the classroom.	
(d)	The library is on the ground floor.	
(e)	There are no computers in the library.	
(f)	Marco often works in the library.	
(g)	There is a door from the library into the garden.	
(h)	The computer room is small and quite dark.	

2. ⌒ Listen to these students talking about their teachers (CD track 30). **(F)**

Is their attitude **P** (positive), **N** (negative) or **P+N** (positive and negative)? Give **one** reason to justify your answer.

	P/N	Reason
1		
2		
3		
4		
5		

4.5 Work and work experience

1. ◯ Listen to these people talking about their work (CD track 31) and complete the table. **(F)**

	Person	Occupation	Opinion
(a)	Alessandro		
(b)	Giulia		
(c)	Gianluca		
(d)	Annamaria		
(e)	Isabella		

2. ▭ Read about the advantages and disadvantages of working from home and answer the following questions. **(H)**

I VANTAGGI DEL TELELAVORO

I vantaggi per i lavoratori
- Grande flessibilità di orario (lavorare nelle ore in cui ci si sente più in forma)
- Necessità ridotta di spostamenti
- Risparmio delle spese
- Riduzione dello stress

I vantaggi per il datore di lavoro
- Maggiore flessibilità d'impiego dei dipendenti
- Retribuzione basata sul lavoro effettivamente svolto
- Taglio delle spese per la gestione di uffici

I vantaggi per la città
- Riduzione del traffico e dell'inquinamento nei centri cittadini

GLI SVANTAGGI DEL TELELAVORO

Ci sono tuttavia alcuni svantaggi.
- Molti si troverebbero all'improvviso senza lavoro (gli operai che producono i mezzi di trasporto, quelli che ne curano la manutenzione, gli autisti, i benzinai e via dicendo)
- Mancanza di contatto umano con i propri colleghi
- Problemi con la tecnologia
- Costi per attrezzature, hardware, software

(a) Give **three** advantages of working from home.

(b) Give **two** advantages for the employer.

(c) What will be the positive outcome for the environment?

(d) Who might suffer from unemployment as a result?

(e) Give **two** problems people who work from home might face.

Part 2: Listening and Reading

1 Out and about

1.1 Visitor information
1(a) C (b) B (c) A (d) C (e) A (f) C
2(a) Austria
 (b) parents
 (c) July 5th
 (d) 10 days
 (e) car
 (f) good
3(a) T (b) F (c) ? (d) F (e) T
 (f) T (g) ? (h) F
4(a) A (b) C (c) B (d) B
5(a) 2.00 a.m./2 in the morning
 (b) winter
 (c) taxi
 (d) apartment/flat
 (e) penguins, koalas and kangaroos
 (f) 100 kilometres

1.2 Basic weather
1(a) A (b) I (c) E (d) B (e) H (f) G
 (g) C (h) F
2(a) Tuesday (b) Sunday (c) Saturday
 (d) Thursday (e) Wednesday

1.3 Local amenities
1(a) 450 (b) 4500 (c) 120
 (d) the beach (e) countryside;
 (f) May
2(a) C (b) B (c) C (d) C (e) A
 (f) B (g) A

1.4 Accommodation
1(a) 2
 (b) 1 double, 1 single
 (c) shower
 (d) 300 euros
 (e) Yes
 (f) 7.00–10.00
2(a) A+B (b) A (c) A (d) B (e) B
 (f) A (g) B (h) A (i) A+B
3(a) 3 (b) 3 (c) two cars
 (d) 300 euros (f) tennis
4(a) A two-storey house, in the
  country.
 (b) When the weather is nice, to have
  dinner.
 (c) Two, one upstairs and one
  downstairs.
 (d) There is a balcony all around.
 (e) It's far from the town/city and
  you have to take the car to go to
  the supermarket.
5(a) F (b) T (c) F (d) ? (e) T

1.5 Public transport
1(a) Return; Venice; 32 euros; 7.25; 3
 (b) Single; Turin; 85 euros; 15.30; 8
 (c) Return; Rome; 64 euros; 18.15;
  13
2(a) S (b) G (c) S (d) N

1.6 Directions
1(a) cross; straight on; right
 (b) traffic lights; left
 (c) on foot; second; in front of.
 (d) crossroads; opposite
2(a) T (b) F (c) ? (d) T (e) F

2 Customer service and transactions

2.1 Cafés and restaurants
1 Correct: (b), (d), (f), (h)
2 Correct: B, D, E, G
3(a) the most important festival
  dedicated to the Neapolitan
  pizza/pizza napoletana
 (b) 11
 (c) beer/limoncello/coffee

2.2 Shops
1(a) shirt (b) 40 (c) light blue
 (d) dark blue (e) 30
2(a) popular; United States
 (b) interest (c) 30%; Germany
 (d) 40%; Sweden (e) 230
3(a) S (b) E (c) L (d) E (e) B
4(a) C (b) H (c) F (d) A
5(a) 32 years, with her husband
 (b) Yes, they have fewer customers.
 (c) working mothers, open until late,
  you can get everything you need
  in the same shop
 (d) Negative outcomes are that lots
  of smaller shops have had to close
  and unemployment has increased.
  On the positive side the
  supermarket has given work to
  young people.
6(a) direct help/assistance
 (b) friends
 (c) impersonal
 (d) older; nearby/in the vicinity

2.3 Dealing with problems
1(a) C (b) F (c) A (d) G (e) B (f) D
2(a) A week ago
 (b) They have come apart at the
  seams
 (c) Another pair
 (d) She doesn't have the receipt
 (e) To have another pair.
3 Correct: (a) (c) (d) (f)

3 Personal information

3.1 General interests
1 1 C
    2 A
    3 D
    4 B
    5 F
2(a) F (b) F (c) M (d) S (e) F
3 1 Positive
    2 Positive + negative
    3 Negative
    4 Positive
    5 Positive + negative
4 Correct answers: (a) (c) (e) (f)
5
Dialogue 1
  (a) About a crazy teacher/about a
      teacher who did silly/crazy
      things.
  (b) It made her laugh, which she
      needed after a stressful day at
      work/in the office.
Dialogue 2
  (a) The actors were very good.
  (b) The plot was too complicated/
      didn't understand anything/too
      long.
Dialogue 3
  (a) She had read the book/liked the
      book.
  (b) She fell asleep before it started/
      didn't see a thing.

3.2 Leisure activities
1(a) playing tennis; in the park; a
     friend
  (b) singing; cultural centre; friends
  (c) watching a football match;
     stadium; Stefano
  (d) going for a walk; in the country;
     friends
  (e) dancing; discotheque; dad/
     husband
  (f) (watching a play); theatre; friend
2(a) C+L (b) C (c) C (d) C+L
  (e) L
3(a) Chloe (b) Eleo (c) Pia (d) Maia
  (e) Lino (f) Guido (g) Maia

3.3 Family and friends
1(a) Simonetta
  (b) 19
  (c) 3 brothers, 1 sister
  (d) Venezuela
  (e) Nice and amusing
2(a) Amanda (b) Engineer
  (c) One year (d) 3 (e) Hotel owner
  (f) None (g) Italian (h) Swiss
3(a) D (b) F (c) H (d) B (e) I (f) C
4(a) F (b) M+F (c) N (d) M (e) N
  (f) F

3.4 Lifestyle (healthy eating and exercise)
1(a) P+N (b) N (c) P (d) N
2(a) Cycling and jogging
  (b) Read lots of books
  (c) Fruit and vegetables
  (d) Fish
3(a) Didn't want to do any sport
  (b) Her boyfriend because she goes
     with him to the gym
  (c) Aerobics twice a week and water
     polo once a week
  (d) Bread and biscuits
  (e) A glass of water with lemon
  (f) Now she only tries healthy things
4 Correct: (a) (d) (e) (h)

4 Future plans, education and work

4.1 Basic language of the internet
1 Correct: (a) (b) (d) (f)
2(a) You can discuss any topic and
     exchange all sorts of information
  (b) Colleagues and strangers
  (c) Soulmates
  (d) He adopts a negative attitude
     because we often don't know
     who we are communicating with
3(a) E (b) G (c) B (d) A (e) D
4(a) You can send messages/book
     plane or train tickets/shop
     without leaving your home
  (b) You can work from home and it's
     less expensive
  (c) You can find out the weather
     forecast and the distance of your
     hotel from the airport
  (d) The elderly as they don't always
     know how to use it
  (e) Back and eyesight problems

4.2 Simple job advertisements
1 (a) D (b) B (c) E (d) A; (e) C
2 (a) Reading job adverts on the internet
 (b) In a museum because she could speak English with the tourists
 (c) A full-time job as it might be too boring
 (d) Earn some money because she would like to travel abroad next year
 (e) She wouldn't want to do it

4.3 Simple job applications and CV
1 Correct: (a) (b) (d) (g)
2 (a) G (b) A (c) D (d) B (e) F

4.4 School and college
1 Correct: (a) (d) (f) (g)
2   1 P; They are nice/intelligent.
     2 N; They are awful/elderly/fat/selfish.
     3 P+N; Sometimes severe, other times nice.
     4 N; They are severe.
     5 P; The teacher is calm.

4.5 Work and work experience
1 (a) doctor; interesting
 (b) unemployed; boring
 (c) office worker; entertaining
 (d) nurse; difficult but satisfying
 (e) housewife; tiring/hard
2 (a) Flexible working hours/less travelling/less expense/reduces stress
 (b) Can use his employees more flexibly/payment based on actual work done/cuts down on office expenditure
 (c) Reduction of traffic and pollution in the city centres
 (d) the workers on the production line, maintenance workers, drivers/service station attendants
 (e) Working harder than when they were in an office/having less free time than they did before

Tracklisting